50 Premium Steak Dinner Recipes

By: Kelly Johnson

Table of Contents

- Filet Mignon with Garlic Butter
- Ribeye Steak with Herb Butter
- New York Strip with Red Wine Reduction
- Tomahawk Steak with Chimichurri Sauce
- Porterhouse Steak with Balsamic Glaze
- T-Bone Steak with Roasted Garlic Compound Butter
- Cowboy Steak with Smoky Bourbon Sauce
- Flat Iron Steak with Blue Cheese Crumbles
- Hanger Steak with Mustard Shallot Sauce
- Flank Steak with Chimichurri Marinade
- Skirt Steak with Spicy Lime Marinade
- Tri-Tip Steak with Coffee Rub
- Bavette Steak with Truffle Butter
- Picanha Steak with Brazilian Marinade
- Denver Steak with Honey Bourbon Glaze
- Sirloin Steak with Peppercorn Sauce
- Chateaubriand with Béarnaise Sauce
- Wagyu Steak with Ponzu Sauce
- Kobe Beef Steak with Miso Butter
- Reverse-Seared Ribeye with Garlic Rosemary Oil
- Sous Vide Filet Mignon with Red Wine Sauce
- Grilled Steak with Roquefort Butter
- Steak au Poivre with Cognac Cream Sauce
- Beef Wellington with Puff Pastry
- Korean BBQ Bulgogi Steak
- Argentinian Asado-Style Steak
- Cajun Blackened Steak
- Steak Diane with Brandy Mushroom Sauce
- Garlic and Herb Marinated Grilled Steak
- Teriyaki Glazed Sirloin Steak
- Mediterranean-Style Steak with Olive Tapenade
- Smoked Brisket-Style Steak
- Thai-Style Grilled Steak with Peanut Sauce
- Balsamic Marinated Hanger Steak
- Steak Frites with Garlic Aioli

- Bourbon and Brown Sugar Marinated Steak
- Gorgonzola-Crusted Steak
- Brazilian Picanha with Sea Salt Crust
- Steak Tartare with Capers and Shallots
- Argentine-Style Churrasco Steak with Salsa Criolla
- Philly Cheesesteak-Style Ribeye
- Grilled Steak with Chimichurri Butter
- Japanese A5 Wagyu with Yuzu Kosho
- Garlic Butter Basted Ribeye
- Lemon and Rosemary Marinated Grilled Steak
- Steak with Wild Mushroom and Truffle Sauce
- Texas-Style Smoked Beef Ribeye
- Mediterranean Steak with Feta and Roasted Peppers
- Miso Marinated Hanger Steak
- Red Wine Braised Short Rib Steak

Filet Mignon with Garlic Butter

Ingredients:

- 2 (6-8 oz) filet mignon steaks
- Salt and freshly ground black pepper, to taste
- 2 tbsp olive oil
- 2 tbsp unsalted butter
- 2 garlic cloves, minced
- 1 tsp fresh rosemary, chopped
- 1 tsp fresh thyme, chopped

Instructions:

1. **Prepare the Steaks:**
   - Remove the filet mignon from the fridge about 30 minutes before cooking to bring them to room temperature.
   - Pat dry with paper towels and season generously with salt and black pepper.
2. **Sear the Steaks:**
   - Heat a cast-iron skillet over medium-high heat and add olive oil.
   - Once hot, add the steaks and sear for about **3-4 minutes per side** for medium-rare (adjust time for desired doneness).
3. **Add Garlic Butter & Herbs:**
   - Reduce heat to medium-low and add butter, minced garlic, rosemary, and thyme.
   - Spoon the melted butter over the steaks for about **1-2 minutes** to enhance the flavor.
4. **Rest & Serve:**
   - Transfer steaks to a plate and let them rest for **5 minutes** before serving.
   - Drizzle remaining garlic butter over the top and enjoy!

Ribeye Steak with Herb Butter

Ingredients:

- 2 (12-14 oz) ribeye steaks
- Salt and freshly ground black pepper, to taste
- 2 tbsp olive oil
- 3 tbsp unsalted butter
- 1 garlic clove, minced
- 1 tsp fresh rosemary, chopped
- 1 tsp fresh thyme, chopped

Instructions:

1. Bring steaks to room temperature and season with salt and pepper.
2. Heat olive oil in a cast-iron skillet over medium-high heat.
3. Sear steaks for **3-4 minutes per side** for medium-rare.
4. Lower heat, add butter, garlic, rosemary, and thyme, basting the steaks for 1-2 minutes.
5. Rest for 5 minutes, then serve with extra herb butter on top.

New York Strip with Red Wine Reduction

Ingredients:

- 2 (10-12 oz) New York strip steaks
- Salt and black pepper, to taste
- 2 tbsp olive oil
- 1/2 cup red wine (Cabernet Sauvignon or Merlot)
- 1/4 cup beef broth
- 1 tbsp unsalted butter
- 1 shallot, finely chopped

Instructions:

1. Season steaks and sear in olive oil over medium-high heat for **3-4 minutes per side**.
2. Remove steaks and let them rest.
3. In the same pan, sauté shallots until soft. Add wine and broth, simmer until reduced by half.
4. Stir in butter and drizzle over steaks.

Tomahawk Steak with Chimichurri Sauce

Ingredients:

- 1 (2-3 lb) tomahawk steak
- Salt and black pepper, to taste
- 2 tbsp olive oil

Chimichurri Sauce:

- 1/2 cup fresh parsley, chopped
- 2 garlic cloves, minced
- 1/4 cup olive oil
- 2 tbsp red wine vinegar
- 1 tsp crushed red pepper flakes
- Salt and black pepper, to taste

Instructions:

1. Preheat grill to **high heat**. Season steak generously.
2. Sear for **4-5 minutes per side**, then move to indirect heat until it reaches desired doneness.
3. Rest for **10 minutes**.
4. Mix all chimichurri ingredients and serve over the steak.

Porterhouse Steak with Balsamic Glaze

Ingredients:

- 1 (24-32 oz) porterhouse steak
- Salt and black pepper, to taste
- 2 tbsp olive oil

Balsamic Glaze:

- 1/2 cup balsamic vinegar
- 1 tbsp honey
- 1 tbsp butter

Instructions:

1. Heat grill to **high heat** and season steak.
2. Grill for **4-5 minutes per side**, then let it rest.
3. Simmer balsamic vinegar and honey until thickened. Stir in butter.
4. Drizzle glaze over the steak before serving.

T-Bone Steak with Roasted Garlic Compound Butter

Ingredients:

- 2 (16-20 oz) T-bone steaks
- Salt and black pepper, to taste
- 2 tbsp olive oil

Roasted Garlic Compound Butter:

- 1/2 cup unsalted butter, softened
- 1 head garlic, roasted and mashed
- 1 tsp fresh thyme, chopped
- 1 tsp fresh rosemary, chopped
- Salt and black pepper, to taste

Instructions:

1. Roast garlic by cutting the top off, drizzling with olive oil, wrapping in foil, and baking at 400°F (200°C) for **30-35 minutes**.
2. Mix roasted garlic with softened butter, herbs, salt, and pepper.
3. Heat grill or skillet to high heat. Season steaks and cook **4-5 minutes per side** for medium-rare.
4. Rest for 5 minutes, then top with garlic butter before serving.

Cowboy Steak with Smoky Bourbon Sauce

Ingredients:

- 1 (2-3 lb) cowboy ribeye steak
- Salt and black pepper, to taste
- 2 tbsp olive oil

Smoky Bourbon Sauce:

- 1/2 cup bourbon
- 1/4 cup beef broth
- 2 tbsp Worcestershire sauce
- 1 tbsp brown sugar
- 1 tbsp butter

Instructions:

1. Heat grill to **high heat** and season steak.
2. Sear for **5-6 minutes per side**, then rest.
3. In a pan, reduce bourbon, broth, Worcestershire, and brown sugar until thick. Stir in butter.
4. Serve sauce over steak.

Flat Iron Steak with Blue Cheese Crumbles

Ingredients:

- 2 (8-10 oz) flat iron steaks
- Salt and black pepper, to taste
- 2 tbsp olive oil
- 1/4 cup blue cheese crumbles

Instructions:

1. Season steaks and sear in a skillet over medium-high heat for **3-4 minutes per side**.
2. Let rest, then top with blue cheese crumbles before serving.

Hanger Steak with Mustard Shallot Sauce

Ingredients:

- 2 (8-10 oz) hanger steaks
- Salt and black pepper, to taste
- 2 tbsp olive oil

Mustard Shallot Sauce:

- 1 shallot, minced
- 1/4 cup Dijon mustard
- 1/4 cup heavy cream
- 1 tbsp butter

Instructions:

1. Sear steaks for **3-4 minutes per side**, then rest.
2. Sauté shallots in butter, stir in mustard and cream. Simmer.
3. Serve sauce over steak.

Flank Steak with Chimichurri Marinade

Ingredients:

- 1 (1.5 lb) flank steak
- Salt and black pepper, to taste

Chimichurri Marinade:

- 1/2 cup fresh parsley, chopped
- 3 tbsp red wine vinegar
- 2 tbsp olive oil
- 2 garlic cloves, minced
- 1 tsp red pepper flakes

Instructions:

1. Marinate steak for **at least 1 hour**.
2. Grill over high heat for **3-4 minutes per side**, then rest.
3. Serve with extra chimichurri.

Skirt Steak with Spicy Lime Marinade

Ingredients:

- 1 (1.5 lb) skirt steak

Spicy Lime Marinade:

- 1/4 cup lime juice
- 2 tbsp olive oil
- 1 tsp chili powder
- 1 tsp cumin
- 2 garlic cloves, minced

Instructions:

1. Marinate steak for **30 minutes**.
2. Grill for **2-3 minutes per side**, then rest.

Tri-Tip Steak with Coffee Rub

Ingredients:

- 1 (2-3 lb) tri-tip steak

Coffee Rub:

- 2 tbsp ground coffee
- 1 tbsp brown sugar
- 1 tsp smoked paprika
- 1 tsp salt
- 1/2 tsp black pepper

Instructions:

1. Coat steak with coffee rub and let sit for **30 minutes**.
2. Grill for **5-6 minutes per side**, then rest.

Bavette Steak with Truffle Butter

Ingredients:

- 2 (8-10 oz) bavette steaks

Truffle Butter:

- 1/2 cup unsalted butter, softened
- 1 tsp truffle oil
- 1/2 tsp salt

Instructions:

1. Cook steak **4-5 minutes per side**, then rest.
2. Top with truffle butter before serving.

Picanha Steak with Brazilian Marinade

Ingredients:

- 1 (2-3 lb) picanha steak

Brazilian Marinade:

- 1/4 cup olive oil
- 3 garlic cloves, minced
- 1 tbsp kosher salt
- 1 tsp black pepper

Instructions:

1. Marinate steak for **1 hour**.
2. Grill for **4-5 minutes per side**, then rest.

Denver Steak with Honey Bourbon Glaze

Ingredients:

- 2 (8-10 oz) Denver steaks
- Salt and black pepper, to taste
- 2 tbsp olive oil

Honey Bourbon Glaze:

- 1/4 cup bourbon
- 2 tbsp honey
- 1 tbsp Dijon mustard
- 1 tbsp soy sauce
- 1 tsp smoked paprika

Instructions:

1. Whisk together glaze ingredients and set aside.
2. Season steaks and grill for **3-4 minutes per side**.
3. Brush with glaze in the last **2 minutes** of cooking.
4. Rest for 5 minutes, then serve.

Sirloin Steak with Peppercorn Sauce

Ingredients:

- 2 (10-12 oz) sirloin steaks
- Salt and black pepper, to taste
- 2 tbsp olive oil

Peppercorn Sauce:

- 1/4 cup brandy or cognac
- 1/2 cup heavy cream
- 1 tbsp black peppercorns, crushed
- 1 tbsp butter

Instructions:

1. Sear steaks for **4-5 minutes per side**, then rest.
2. Deglaze pan with brandy, add peppercorns and cream, and simmer until thick.
3. Stir in butter and serve over steaks.

Chateaubriand with Béarnaise Sauce

Ingredients:

- 1 (1.5-2 lb) center-cut beef tenderloin
- Salt and black pepper, to taste
- 2 tbsp olive oil

Béarnaise Sauce:

- 1/4 cup white wine vinegar
- 1 shallot, minced
- 2 egg yolks
- 1/2 cup unsalted butter, melted
- 1 tbsp fresh tarragon, chopped

Instructions:

1. Sear tenderloin on all sides, then roast at **400°F (200°C) for 15-20 minutes**.
2. Simmer vinegar and shallots, whisk in egg yolks, then slowly add melted butter.
3. Stir in tarragon and serve with steak.

Wagyu Steak with Ponzu Sauce

Ingredients:

- 2 (6-8 oz) Wagyu steaks
- Salt and black pepper, to taste

Ponzu Sauce:

- 1/4 cup soy sauce
- 2 tbsp fresh lime juice
- 1 tbsp mirin
- 1 tsp grated ginger

Instructions:

1. Sear Wagyu for **1-2 minutes per side** over high heat.
2. Drizzle with ponzu sauce before serving.

Kobe Beef Steak with Miso Butter

Ingredients:

- 2 (6-8 oz) Kobe beef steaks

Miso Butter:

- 1/4 cup unsalted butter, softened
- 1 tbsp white miso paste
- 1 tsp soy sauce

Instructions:

1. Cook steaks for **1-2 minutes per side**.
2. Top with miso butter before serving.

Reverse-Seared Ribeye with Garlic Rosemary Oil

Ingredients:

- 1 (16-20 oz) ribeye steak

Garlic Rosemary Oil:

- 1/4 cup olive oil
- 2 garlic cloves, minced
- 1 tsp fresh rosemary, chopped

Instructions:

1. Roast steak at **225°F (107°C) until it reaches 115°F (46°C) internal temp**.
2. Sear in a hot skillet for **1-2 minutes per side**.
3. Drizzle with garlic rosemary oil before serving.

Sous Vide Filet Mignon with Red Wine Sauce

Ingredients:

- 2 (6-8 oz) filet mignon steaks

Red Wine Sauce:

- 1/2 cup red wine
- 1/4 cup beef broth
- 1 shallot, minced
- 1 tbsp butter

Instructions:

1. Sous vide steaks at **130°F (54°C) for 1-2 hours**.
2. Sear in a hot pan for **1 minute per side**.
3. Reduce wine, broth, and shallots in a pan, then stir in butter. Serve over steaks.

Grilled Steak with Roquefort Butter

Ingredients:

- 2 (10-12 oz) steaks

Roquefort Butter:

- 1/4 cup Roquefort cheese
- 2 tbsp butter, softened

Instructions:

1. Grill steaks for **4-5 minutes per side**.
2. Top with Roquefort butter before serving.

Steak au Poivre with Cognac Cream Sauce

Ingredients:

- 2 (8-10 oz) steaks

Cognac Cream Sauce:

- 1/4 cup cognac
- 1/2 cup heavy cream
- 1 tbsp butter

Instructions:

1. Coat steaks in crushed peppercorns and sear.
2. Deglaze with cognac, add cream, and stir in butter.

Beef Wellington with Puff Pastry

Ingredients:

- 1 (2 lb) beef tenderloin
- Salt and black pepper, to taste
- 2 tbsp olive oil
- 8 oz mushrooms, finely chopped
- 1/4 cup Dijon mustard
- 6 slices prosciutto
- 1 sheet puff pastry
- 1 egg, beaten

Instructions:

1. Sear beef on all sides, then coat with mustard.
2. Sauté mushrooms, then layer prosciutto and mushrooms around beef.
3. Wrap in puff pastry, brush with egg wash, and bake at **400°F (200°C) for 25-30 minutes**.

Korean BBQ Bulgogi Steak

Ingredients:

- 1 lb ribeye or sirloin steak, thinly sliced
- 1/4 cup soy sauce
- 2 tbsp brown sugar
- 2 tbsp sesame oil
- 2 garlic cloves, minced
- 1 tsp grated ginger
- 1 tbsp rice vinegar
- 1/2 tsp red pepper flakes
- 2 green onions, chopped
- 1 tbsp toasted sesame seeds

Instructions:

1. Mix all marinade ingredients in a bowl and add sliced steak. Marinate for **at least 1 hour**.
2. Heat a skillet or grill over high heat. Cook steak for **2-3 minutes per side**.
3. Garnish with green onions and sesame seeds before serving.

Argentinian Asado-Style Steak

Ingredients:

- 2 (12-14 oz) bone-in ribeye or skirt steaks
- Salt and black pepper, to taste

Chimichurri Sauce:

- 1/2 cup fresh parsley, chopped
- 3 tbsp red wine vinegar
- 2 tbsp olive oil
- 2 garlic cloves, minced
- 1 tsp red pepper flakes

Instructions:

1. Season steaks with salt and black pepper.
2. Grill over an open flame for **4-5 minutes per side** for medium-rare.
3. Serve with chimichurri sauce.

Cajun Blackened Steak

Ingredients:

- 2 (10-12 oz) New York strip or ribeye steaks
- 2 tbsp olive oil

Cajun Spice Rub:

- 1 tbsp smoked paprika
- 1 tsp cayenne pepper
- 1 tsp garlic powder
- 1 tsp onion powder
- 1 tsp black pepper
- 1 tsp salt

Instructions:

1. Coat steaks with Cajun spice rub.
2. Sear in a hot skillet for **2-3 minutes per side**, then reduce heat and cook to desired doneness.
3. Rest for 5 minutes before serving.

Steak Diane with Brandy Mushroom Sauce

Ingredients:

- 2 (8-10 oz) filet mignon or sirloin steaks
- Salt and black pepper, to taste
- 2 tbsp butter
- 1 shallot, minced
- 1/2 cup mushrooms, sliced
- 1/4 cup brandy
- 1/2 cup heavy cream
- 1 tsp Dijon mustard

Instructions:

1. Sear steaks for **3-4 minutes per side**, then remove from pan.
2. Sauté shallots and mushrooms in butter. Add brandy and flambé.
3. Stir in cream and Dijon mustard. Serve sauce over steak.

Garlic and Herb Marinated Grilled Steak

Ingredients:

- 2 (12 oz) ribeye or sirloin steaks

Marinade:

- 1/4 cup olive oil
- 3 garlic cloves, minced
- 1 tsp fresh rosemary, chopped
- 1 tsp fresh thyme, chopped
- 1 tbsp lemon juice
- Salt and black pepper, to taste

Instructions:

1. Marinate steaks for **at least 2 hours**.
2. Grill for **4-5 minutes per side**.
3. Let rest before serving.

Teriyaki Glazed Sirloin Steak

Ingredients:

- 2 (10-12 oz) sirloin steaks

Teriyaki Glaze:

- 1/4 cup soy sauce
- 2 tbsp honey
- 1 tbsp rice vinegar
- 1 tsp grated ginger
- 1 garlic clove, minced

Instructions:

1. Marinate steak for **30 minutes**.
2. Grill for **4-5 minutes per side**, brushing with extra glaze.

Mediterranean-Style Steak with Olive Tapenade

Ingredients:

- 2 (10-12 oz) flank or sirloin steaks

Olive Tapenade:

- 1/2 cup mixed olives, chopped
- 2 tbsp capers
- 1 tbsp lemon juice
- 1 tbsp olive oil
- 1 garlic clove, minced

Instructions:

1. Season and grill steaks for **4-5 minutes per side**.
2. Mix tapenade ingredients and serve over steak.

Smoked Brisket-Style Steak

Ingredients:

- 1 (2-3 lb) brisket or chuck steak

Rub:

- 2 tbsp smoked paprika
- 1 tbsp brown sugar
- 1 tsp black pepper
- 1 tsp salt
- 1/2 tsp cayenne

Instructions:

1. Rub steak with spices and smoke at **225°F (107°C) for 3-4 hours**.
2. Wrap in foil and continue smoking until tender.

Thai-Style Grilled Steak with Peanut Sauce

Ingredients:

- 2 (8-10 oz) skirt or flank steaks

Peanut Sauce:

- 1/4 cup peanut butter
- 2 tbsp soy sauce
- 1 tbsp lime juice
- 1 tsp sriracha

Instructions:

1. Grill steak for **3-4 minutes per side**.
2. Serve with peanut sauce.

Balsamic Marinated Hanger Steak

Ingredients:

- 2 (8-10 oz) hanger steaks

Balsamic Marinade:

- 1/4 cup balsamic vinegar
- 2 tbsp olive oil
- 1 tbsp Dijon mustard
- 2 garlic cloves, minced

Instructions:

1. Marinate steaks for **1-2 hours**.
2. Grill for **4-5 minutes per side**.

Steak Frites with Garlic Aioli

Ingredients:

- 2 (10-12 oz) New York strip or ribeye steaks
- Salt and black pepper, to taste
- 2 tbsp olive oil

Frites:

- 2 large russet potatoes, cut into fries
- 2 tbsp olive oil
- Salt, to taste

Garlic Aioli:

- 1/2 cup mayonnaise
- 2 garlic cloves, minced
- 1 tbsp lemon juice

Instructions:

1. Toss fries with olive oil and bake at **425°F (220°C) for 25-30 minutes**.
2. Grill steaks for **4-5 minutes per side**, then rest.
3. Mix aioli ingredients and serve with fries.

Bourbon and Brown Sugar Marinated Steak

Ingredients:

- 2 (12 oz) ribeye or sirloin steaks

Marinade:

- 1/4 cup bourbon
- 2 tbsp brown sugar
- 1 tbsp Worcestershire sauce
- 1 tsp smoked paprika

Instructions:

1. Marinate steaks for **2 hours**.
2. Grill for **4-5 minutes per side**.

Gorgonzola-Crusted Steak

Ingredients:

- 2 (10 oz) filet mignon or ribeye steaks

Gorgonzola Crust:

- 1/4 cup gorgonzola cheese
- 2 tbsp butter, softened
- 1/4 cup panko breadcrumbs

Instructions:

1. Cook steaks for **4-5 minutes per side**.
2. Mix crust ingredients and broil on steaks for **1-2 minutes**.

Brazilian Picanha with Sea Salt Crust

Ingredients:

- 1 (2-3 lb) picanha steak
- 2 tbsp coarse sea salt

Instructions:

1. Generously season steak with sea salt.
2. Grill over open flame for **5-6 minutes per side**.

Steak Tartare with Capers and Shallots

Ingredients:

- 8 oz high-quality beef, finely chopped
- 1 egg yolk
- 1 tbsp capers, chopped
- 1 tbsp shallots, minced
- 1 tsp Dijon mustard
- 1 tsp Worcestershire sauce

Instructions:

1. Mix all ingredients in a bowl.
2. Serve with toast or crackers.

Argentine-Style Churrasco Steak with Salsa Criolla

Ingredients:

- 2 (12 oz) skirt or flank steaks

Salsa Criolla:

- 1/2 cup red bell pepper, diced
- 1/4 cup red onion, diced
- 2 tbsp olive oil
- 1 tbsp red wine vinegar

Instructions:

1. Grill steaks for **4-5 minutes per side**.
2. Mix salsa ingredients and serve on top.

Philly Cheesesteak-Style Ribeye

Ingredients:

- 2 (10-12 oz) ribeye steaks, thinly sliced
- 1/2 cup sautéed onions
- 1/2 cup bell peppers, sliced
- 4 slices provolone cheese
- 2 hoagie rolls

Instructions:

1. Cook ribeye slices in a hot skillet.
2. Top with onions, peppers, and cheese, then serve in hoagie rolls.

Grilled Steak with Chimichurri Butter

Ingredients:

- 2 (12 oz) sirloin or ribeye steaks

Chimichurri Butter:

- 1/4 cup unsalted butter, softened
- 2 tbsp chimichurri sauce

Instructions:

1. Grill steaks for **4-5 minutes per side**.
2. Top with chimichurri butter before serving.

Japanese A5 Wagyu with Yuzu Kosho

Ingredients:

- 2 (6-8 oz) A5 Wagyu steaks
- 1 tsp yuzu kosho (Japanese citrus chili paste)
- Sea salt, to taste

Instructions:

1. Sear Wagyu for **1-2 minutes per side**.
2. Serve with yuzu kosho and sea salt.

Garlic Butter Basted Ribeye

Ingredients:

- 2 (12-14 oz) ribeye steaks
- Salt and black pepper, to taste
- 2 tbsp olive oil
- 4 tbsp unsalted butter
- 3 garlic cloves, crushed
- 2 sprigs fresh rosemary

Instructions:

1. Heat a cast-iron skillet over high heat.
2. Sear steaks for **3-4 minutes per side**.
3. Reduce heat to medium, add butter, garlic, and rosemary. Baste steaks for **1-2 minutes**.
4. Rest for 5 minutes before serving.

Lemon and Rosemary Marinated Grilled Steak

Ingredients:

- 2 (10-12 oz) sirloin or flank steaks

Marinade:

- 1/4 cup olive oil
- 2 tbsp lemon juice
- 1 tbsp fresh rosemary, chopped
- 2 garlic cloves, minced
- Salt and black pepper, to taste

Instructions:

1. Marinate steaks for **at least 1 hour**.
2. Grill over medium-high heat for **4-5 minutes per side**.

Steak with Wild Mushroom and Truffle Sauce

Ingredients:

- 2 (10-12 oz) filet mignon or ribeye steaks

Mushroom Truffle Sauce:

- 1 cup mixed wild mushrooms, sliced
- 1/4 cup heavy cream
- 1 tbsp truffle oil
- 1/4 cup beef broth
- 1 tbsp butter

Instructions:

1. Cook steaks for **4-5 minutes per side**, then rest.
2. Sauté mushrooms in butter, add broth, then stir in cream and truffle oil.
3. Serve sauce over steak.

Texas-Style Smoked Beef Ribeye

Ingredients:

- 1 (2-3 lb) bone-in ribeye steak

Dry Rub:

- 1 tbsp smoked paprika
- 1 tbsp coarse salt
- 1 tbsp black pepper
- 1 tsp garlic powder

Instructions:

1. Rub steak with seasoning and let sit for **30 minutes**.
2. Smoke at **225°F (107°C) for 1.5-2 hours** until internal temp reaches 125°F (52°C).
3. Sear over high heat for **1-2 minutes per side**.

Mediterranean Steak with Feta and Roasted Peppers

Ingredients:

- 2 (10-12 oz) flank or sirloin steaks

Topping:

- 1/2 cup feta cheese, crumbled
- 1/4 cup roasted red peppers, chopped
- 1 tbsp olive oil

Instructions:

1. Grill steaks for **4-5 minutes per side**.
2. Mix feta, peppers, and olive oil, then serve over steak.

Miso Marinated Hanger Steak

Ingredients:

- 2 (8-10 oz) hanger steaks

Miso Marinade:

- 2 tbsp white miso paste
- 1 tbsp soy sauce
- 1 tbsp rice vinegar
- 1 tsp grated ginger

Instructions:

1. Marinate steak for **1 hour**.
2. Grill over high heat for **4-5 minutes per side**.

Red Wine Braised Short Rib Steak

Ingredients:

- 2 (12 oz) bone-in short rib steaks
- Salt and black pepper, to taste
- 1 tbsp olive oil
- 1 cup red wine
- 1/2 cup beef broth
- 1 onion, chopped
- 2 garlic cloves, minced

Instructions:

1. Sear steaks in a Dutch oven over medium-high heat.
2. Add onions and garlic, then deglaze with red wine and broth.
3. Cover and braise at **325°F (163°C) for 2-3 hours**.

www.ingramcontent.com/pod-product-compliance
Lightning Source LLC
LaVergne TN
LVHW081501060526
838201LV00056BA/2870